Coping™

COPING WITH
GUN VIOLENCE

Tiffanie Drayton

Rosen
YA™

New York

Published in 2019 by The Rosen Publishing Group, Inc.
29 East 21st Street, New York, NY 10010

First Edition

Library of Congress Cataloging-in-Publication Data

Names: Drayton, Tiffanie, author.
Title: Coping with gun violence / Tiffanie Drayton.
Description: First edition. | New York : Rosen Publishing, 2019. | Series: Coping | Includes bibliographical references and index. | Audience: Grades 7–12.
Identifiers: LCCN 2018015266| ISBN 9781508183198 (library bound) | ISBN 9781499467161 (pbk.)
Subjects: LCSH: Firearms and crime—United States—Juvenile literature. | Violent crimes—United States—Juvenile literature. | Firearms accidents—United States—Juvenile literataure. | Mass shootings—United States—Juvenile literature. | Gun control—United States—Juvenile literature.
Classification: LCC HV7436 .D73 2019 | DDC 362.88—dc23
LC record available at https://lccn.loc.gov/2018015266

Manufactured in China

CONTENTS

INTRODUCTION

Timea Batts, a sixth grader from Nashville, Tennessee, was excited to get home after a long first day of school. She boarded the bus home from Knox Doss Middle School on August 8, 2016, dressed in the new clothes bought by her father during their back-to-school shopping trip only a few days earlier. Sadly, Timea's first day of school would be the last day of her life. Within moments of getting off the school bus and entering her home, Timea's father mistook her for an intruder and shot her in their home. A security camera caught the details of the awful accident. It showed Timea walking into her home, taking off her shoes and backpack, and then quietly walking through the house. Reportedly, she snuck up on her father and screamed "roar." Startled and scared, he pulled out a handgun and fired one shot. The bullet went through her chest, came out the other side, and lodged in the wall. Timea Batts died on the way to the hospital.

"Daddy, I know it was an accident," she told her father on the way to the emergency room.

Sadly, Timea Batts's story is not uncommon. *The Future of Children* journal reports that more than twenty thousand children and teens younger than age twenty lose their lives or are injured because of gun violence every year. Many, like Timea, are shot and killed by friends or even family. Such tragedies are

This child's casket is covered with roses and a stuffed bear. The CDC reported that twenty-six thousand children and teens were killed by guns in the United States between 1996 and 2016.

particularly common in the United States, which has more gun-related violence than most other countries. According to the Congressional Research Services, there are more guns in America than people, and that number is steadily increasing every year.

Gun violence takes a major toll on society. Every year, hundreds of billions of dollars are spent on medical expenses to treat injuries caused by firearms, on legal fees for court cases where guns are used in crimes, and on other expenses related to gun violence. Gun violence can come in the form of accidental shootings, suicide, homicide, violent robbery, and assault. It can also lead to psychological trauma. Whether people witness gun violence in the media or face it in their own lives, many people need help dealing with the fear, anxiety, and pain that it causes.

If you are experiencing fear, trauma, or anxiety because of gun violence, there are ways to cope with these feelings. Moreover, by learning about the issues that lead to gun violence, it is possible for people across the country, and from all walks of life, to work together to change the culture in which gun violence thrives. Through research, advocacy, community involvement, education, and awareness, Americans can create safer schools and communities for everyone.

CHAPTER ONE

What Is Gun Violence?

Gun violence is any violence committed with the use of a firearm. It can be classified in two ways: criminal or noncriminal. Gun violence can be noncriminal if an incident involving a firearm is an accident and results in death or injury. However, other types of gun violence are considered crimes. Suicide, homicide (unless it is deemed justified), and assault with a deadly weapon are all examples of criminal gun violence that can carry heavy penalties in court and result in prosecution and incarceration.

While many people imagine that the majority of guns in the world are controlled by the police or military, the truth is that civilians control the lion's share of firearms. According to GunPolicy. org, there are approximately 875 million guns in the world, and 75 percent of them are civilian owned. This estimate is likely conservative

Levels of gun violence are particularly high in the United States because of the widespread availability of firearms.

because it is almost impossible to account for every firearm in distribution. There are also many illegal guns in the world, and the manufacturing of firearms continues to be extremely profitable, creating high demand and thus high production. Civilian ownership of guns is an international phenomenon, but the United States has the highest rates of gun ownership in the world. According to the Small Arms Survey, Americans own approximately 42 percent of the world's guns. A 2009 National Institute of Justice report found that there were about 310 million firearms in circulation in the United States.

Unsurprisingly, civilian possession of these dangerous weapons has major ramifications. Gun homicide rates in the United States are 25.2 times higher than any other industrialized nation, according to a 2010 study in the *American Journal of Medicine.*

Between 1966 and 2012, there were ninety public mass shootings in the United States, compared to ten in France and eleven in the Philippines. Every day, an average of ninety-six Americans are killed by guns and many more are injured, according to the Centers for Disease Control and Prevention (CDC).

Accidental Gun-Related Deaths

If a shooter does not intentionally mean to cause harm but death results from the use of a firearm, it is classified as an accidental death. Statistics compiled by the CDC reveal that there were 130,557 deaths from unintentional injuries in 2013, making it the fourth-ranked cause of death overall. A study based on data from 2012 to 2014 estimated that, on average, 5,790 children in the United States receive medical treatment in an emergency room each year for a gun-related injury. About 21 percent of those injuries are unintentional. During that same time period, an average of 1,297 children died annually from a gun-related injury in the United States. In the vast majority of accidental firearm deaths among youth, the gunshot wound was either self-inflicted or at the hands of another child.

Guns found in the home are used in many accidental death shootings. According to the Brady Center's report "The Truth About Kids & Guns," one

A grieving woman holds flowers during a funeral service. Tens of thousands of people lose loved ones to gun violence every year in the United States.

out of three homes with kids have guns in them, and 1.7 million children live in homes with unlocked, loaded guns. Easy access to firearms has claimed the lives of millions of children worldwide and is one of the most preventable types of violence. There is a strong connection between gun availability and rates of death for children. States where it is easy to access a firearm have significantly higher rates of death from gunshots for children compared to states where guns are less available. Studies have also found that states that have implemented Child Access Prevention (CAP) laws have lower rates of unintentional deaths compared to states that do not have such laws.

Suicide

Everyone experiences moments in life when they feel overwhelmed, sad, and unable to cope. For some people, these feelings are so intense that they may try to take their own lives. Access to guns exacerbates these saddening circumstances. Data from the CDC estimates that about fifty-eight Americans take their lives with guns every day. The CDC also reports that suicide is the second-leading cause of death among teens between the ages of fifteen and nineteen. Most teens who attempt suicide suffer from mental health issues, including mood disorders like depression and bipolar disorder. A study by the *Journal of Clinical*

Psychiatry found that more than 90 percent of children and adolescents who committed or attempted suicide had been diagnosed with a mental health problem. While teen girls are just about twice as likely to try to take their own lives, teen boys are more likely to complete a suicide attempt. In 2014, firearms were used in 41 percent of all teen suicides.

CDC data shows that suicide with a gun is by far the deadliest method. In fact, the majority of gun deaths in the United States (more than twenty-one thousand annually) are suicides involving a firearm. Just the availability and presence of a gun in the home is a strong predictor of gun-assisted suicide. Research has established that oftentimes a person may try to commit suicide in an impulsive act, but survivors of a first attempt rarely try to end their lives again. Sadly, if a suicide attempt involves a gun, there is much less of a chance of survival. While it may be impossible to stop people from attempting to take their lives in times of distress, limiting access to deadly weapons is crucial to reducing the number of successful suicides.

Domestic Violence

Gun availability makes the Unites States a particularly dangerous place for women. A study published in the *American Journal of Medicine* found that women in the United States are sixteen times more likely to be shot and killed in a domestic violence incident than anywhere else in the developed world. In a typical month, fifty American women are shot to death by their intimate partners. Every year, American women are impacted by 5.3 million incidents of domestic abuse, and when their abusers have guns, there is a significantly increased likelihood that this abuse will lead to death. Guns are also used to intimidate and control victims in domestic violence situations, even if the trigger is never pulled. Nearly one million women alive today have been threatened with a gun by domestic abusers.

Domestic violence comes at a huge societal cost. More than $8 billion is spent every year to cover the costs incurred by domestic violence. These costs include medical bills, mental health bills, and the loss sustained by the economy when victims are unable to work due to injuries inflicted on them in domestic violence incidents. Domestic violence leads to 13.5 million days of lost work every year, according to Everytown for Gun Safety.

Gun laws save the lives of many women who face intimate partner violence. In 1998, the National Instant Criminal Background

The presence of a gun in the house makes domestic violence situations much more dangerous and potentially fatal.

Check System (NICS) was launched by the Federal Bureau of Investigation (FBI), mandating criminal background checks before a gun purchase. This law restricts people with an official record of domestic violence from purchasing firearms. According to the US Department of Justice, background checks have stopped more than three hundred thousand domestic abusers from getting their hands on guns, saving thousands of lives. One in seven people blocked from purchasing a gun is a domestic abuser.

Sadly, these measures taken by the federal government do not stop all domestic abusers from accessing guns. Federal gun laws have their limitations, especially when it comes to implementation. While nineteen states require extensive background checks on all handgun sales, there are still many states where abusers can avoid passing a background check if they purchase the weapon from an unlicensed seller. It is also up to the state to ensure that people charged with domestic violence hand in any guns they own, but these measures are not always taken. Sometimes, a state may not have the necessary funds or capacity to enforce federal law.

Robbery and Assault

Ronald Espinoza and Alex Diaz were only fourteen and fifteen years old when they entered an electronics store in Queens, New York, armed with guns. A struggle ensued when Diaz went behind the counter to try to steal money and was met with resistance from the shop's owner. The pair of teens hit the thirty-eight-year-old owner in the head with their guns multiple times and tried to cut him with a knife. The shop owner's wife was also attacked when she tried to step in. Luckily, the owner's daughter escaped to the basement and alerted authorities. Police officers arrived on the scene, but the teens had already fled. They were eventually cornered and arrested at a subway station. Police officers recovered three guns and stolen property. Diaz and Espinoza were charged with robbery, assault, criminal use of a firearm, and criminal possession of a weapon.

It is very scary to become a victim of a violent crime, especially if your life is threatened by deadly weapons. According to the National Crime Victimization survey, between 1993 and 2001, approximately 26 percent of the average 8.9 million violent victimizations that occur every year were committed by criminals armed with a weapon. Of those violent victimizations, 10 percent involved guns. On a positive note, the report also found a 63 percent decrease in violence committed with firearms in that nine-year period. Still, every day, people's lives are threatened by criminals who feel fearless and empowered because they are carrying a powerful weapon.

The Death of Hadiya Pendleton

On January 29, 2013, Hadiya Pendleton, a fifteen-year-old girl from Chicago, was shot in the back while standing in a neighborhood park, only moments after completing her final exams at King College Prep High School. Two other students were injured in the shooting and survived, but Hadiya died within moments of being struck. Weeks earlier, the teen had performed at events for President Barack Obama's second inauguration. When suspects Michael Ward (eighteen) and Kenneth Williams (twenty) were arrested and charged with her murder, they admitted to officers that they mistook the group of teens

First Lady Michelle Obama stands with Hadiya Pendleton's mother, Cleopatra Cowley-Pendleton, during President Obama's State of the Union Address.

for rival gang members. The tragic murder sparked national outrage and brought attention to Chicago's ongoing problem with gun violence. Michelle Obama attended Hadiya Pendleton's funeral and President Obama mentioned the teen's death in his 2013 State of the Union address to Congress.

Homicide

When gun violence by one person results in the death of another, it is classified as homicide (except in the case of an accident). Gun-related homicide is the third-leading cause of death among teens, according to the CDC. The types of gun-related homicides that are most commonly reported in the media are mass shootings and police-related shootings, but those are actually not the most common types of gun homicide. Mass shootings account for less than 1 percent of homicides in the United States, and police shootings are also relatively uncommon compared to other types of gun-related homicide. According to the FBI's National Gang Threat Assessment, gang violence accounts for an average of 48 percent of violent crime in most jurisdictions, and up to 90 percent in others. Reports indicate that the majority of gang-related crime is committed with guns.

It is estimated that there are approximately 1.4 million active gang members and more than 33,000 gangs in the United States. These gangs tend to aggressively recruit members from marginalized communities who are vulnerable, oftentimes presenting the gang as a kind of extended family. Teens, undocumented immigrants, and minorities are all prime targets for recruitment by gang leaders. In the 1990s, juvenile gang-related violence committed with guns became more common and widespread. Gang membership continues to increase, and reports of gangs getting their hands on more powerful guns spells serious trouble for teens who find themselves caught up in gang life, not to mention everyone else in their communities. Many gang members are not properly trained to handle these weapons, making them more likely to accidentally harm themselves or innocent bystanders.

Author Sudhir Venkatesh wrote in a *New York Times* article titled "Understanding Kids, Gangs and Guns:"

> *Until I started observing gangs and criminals, I used to think that young, violent criminals were generally adept in gun use. I learned the reality was far worse. Gangs and drug crews had caches of high-powered weapons but no formal training. Their members could not match a gun to its proper bullet. Few knew how to load, clean or shoot. Their aim was woeful: they injured one another—not to mention bystanders—as often as their enemies.*

Youth do not have to be involved in gangs to become victims of gun-related homicide. Young people are the most likely demographic to be both perpetrators of violent crime and victims of it. When there was a huge spike in crime in the 1980s and early 1990s, much of the increase was attributed to crimes committed by

Protesters hold signs during a gun control rally demanding government intervention to end mass shootings.

people younger than twenty. Youth gun-related homicides also spiked during that time period because many young people got their hands on guns and used them during fights or other violent encounters that may have otherwise not turned deadly. After law enforcement cracked down on youth access to guns, those numbers decreased. Nevertheless, many young people still have access to guns, increasing the likelihood that a simple teen squabble can end in death.

CHAPTER TWO

Who Is at Risk?

Everytown for Gun Safety, a nonpartisan organization dedicated to reducing gun violence, reports that Americans are twenty-five times more likely to be murdered with a gun than people in other developed countries due to the prevalence of guns and lax gun-control laws. The University of Washington's Institute for Health Metrics and Evaluation reported 3.85 deaths due to gun violence per 100,000 people in the United States in 2016. That death rate was eight times higher than the rate in Canada, which had 0.48 deaths per 100,000 people, and twenty-seven times higher than the rate in Denmark, which had 0.14 deaths per 100,000 people. The United States has a serious gun violence issue.

According to Politifact, the number of deaths caused by firearms in the United States between the years 1968 and 2011 was actually higher than

Seven-year-old Leslie Espada cries at the funeral of her two-year-old brother, David Pacheco Jr., who was killed by a stray bullet in the Bronx in 2006.

the combined death toll in all the wars ever fought in American history. According to this research, there were about 1.4 million deaths caused by firearms in that forty-three-year span, compared with 1.2 million deaths of American citizens in every war the country had fought, starting with the American Revolution and ending with the Iraq war.

While all lives can potentially be impacted by gun violence, certain factors increase a person's likelihood of exposure. Homes with guns in them pose a very serious danger to children and adolescents, who are more likely than children living in homes without guns to die from self-inflicted gunshots or shots fired by another young person. Black youth also face alarming rates of gun violence in their communities, and rural communities are entrenched with gun-related violence that often goes overlooked by the media.

A Home with Guns Is an Unsafe Home

In the United States, firearm injury is one of the leading causes of death among children ages five to fourteen, according to a 2017 article in *Pediatrics* journal. Guns not only kill children, but they also can cause serious bodily injury. Many of these injuries happen when children access firearms in the home.

Keeping guns in the home often leads to accidental injury or death. It is especially dangerous to store an unlocked gun in a place where children can find it.

One-third of kids live in a home with a firearm present and in more than 40 percent of these gun-owning homes, guns are stored unlocked, according to the Brady Center. Children and teens with firearms in the home are more likely to experience gun-related injury, trauma, or death. Gun-owning parents may believe their children are unaware of a gun kept in the home or believe that they do not touch or come into contact with the weapon, but studies reveal children are far more likely to access the guns in their homes than many families would like to believe.

A study published by Dr. Frances Baxley, based on self-reported information from parents and children, found that 73 percent of children younger than ten who lived in a house with guns reported knowing the gun's storage location, and 36 percent of these youth reported having touched or handled the weapon. One-third of the parents who reported that their child did not know where the firearm was stored in the home and one-fifth of the parents who reported that their child had never held a gun were contradicted by their children's reports.

Sadly, children in the United States are more likely to die of a firearm-related injury than children in any other industrialized country in the world. A study by the *American Journal of Medicine* found that the unintentional firearm-related death rate is nine times higher in the United States than in most other developed countries. There is a strong correlation between gun-related deaths and the presence of firearms in the home, regardless of storage practice, type, or number of guns.

The Tragic Deaths of Kyree and Keon Myers

Kyree Myers was only two years old when he found a loaded gun in his Columbia, South Carolina, home on September 8, 2017. Likely unaware of the real-life dangers of the weapon, he pulled the trigger and shot himself in the head. After the shooting, his distraught mother called 911 and alerted authorities.

When police officers arrived on the scene, Kyree's devastated father, Keon Myers, had a loaded gun pointed at his head and was threatening to take his own life. The police tried to diffuse the situation, but to no avail. Keon Myers fired a single gunshot that struck him in the head. Both Kyree and Keon Myers were rushed to the hospital but succumbed to their injuries. A mother lost her child and her husband on the same day because of a single, loaded gun.

Impact of Gun Violence on Black Children

According to the National Survey of Children's Exposure to Violence, black kids are ten times more likely than white kids to die by gun violence. Gun violence in urban communities is related to high concentrations of poverty and low levels of education and is directly connected to the legacy of racism and discrimination. For the greater part of the twentieth century, racial housing covenants, discriminatory lending practices, and white flight led to de facto housing segregation. A practice known as redlining created literal lines of segregation and pockets of poverty, due to the enforcement of discriminatory banking practices that drew figurative "red lines" around areas where black people were not allowed to apply for mortgages. This practice created concentrated poverty and typically prevented black people from living in safe, suburban neighborhoods,

The phrase "Hands Up, Don't Shoot" was popularized by activists after the death of Michael Brown, who was shot and killed by police while his hands were raised.

forcing them into crime-filled urban environments. The connection between gun violence and poverty in urban communities, and its roots in racism, have been well documented.

Case Study: Gun Violence in Baltimore

In the 1950s, Baltimore was in the midst of an economic slump. Jobs that made the city an economic powerhouse had begun to disappear, and the construction of the city's first highway resulted in white flight, in which white families left the city for suburbs that had become more easily accessible. Riots in the sixties, sparked by the murder of Martin Luther King Jr., also contributed to white families leaving the city in droves. Black people, however, were left behind. Denied access to mortgages by banks that practiced redlining and also denied equal employment opportunity, black people who remained in Baltimore became among the most disenfranchised in the entire nation. Politicians also endorsed segregation plans that prevented black people from moving to white neighborhoods, essentially restricting black people to certain areas of the inner city.

Fast forward to the twenty-first century and many parts of the city are overridden with poverty, unemployment, lack of access to education, and of course, gun violence. In 2015, gun homicides spiked, leaving the city with its highest-ever recorded murder rate per capita, according to data prepared by the Maryland State Police. Much of this violence is concentrated in areas where people are the most disenfranchised. For example, in the neighborhood of Sandtown-Winchester, 60 percent of residents have not earned a high school diploma. Unsurprisingly, this neighborhood is among those with the highest rates of violent crime in the city.

The growing number of homicides remain concentrated in black neighborhoods, with largely white neighborhoods almost completely exempt from the violence. According to local police department statistics, 92 percent of Baltimore's gun murder victims in 2015 were black men. Baltimore's history of racism continues to plague the city and has created crime hotspots that endanger the lives of countless black residents. Similarly, black communities across the country remain impoverished and cut off from opportunity, resulting in increased incidences of crime and gun violence.

Gun Violence in Rural Areas

Guns are most prevalent in rural areas of the United States. According to the Pew Research Center, 46 percent of people who live in rural areas report owning

These two hunters carry shotguns—a common sight in rural America, where 46 percent of people report owning guns.

a gun, compared with 28 percent of suburban-dwelling adults and 19 percent of those who live in urban communities. Many people who live in rural communities own guns for hunting and sometimes receive their first firearm well before their eighteenth birthday. Many rural gun owners view gun ownership as an inalienable right that is essential to their personal sense of freedom.

With the widespread ownership of guns in rural communities, it is no surprise that youth in these communities are at risk of accidental injury or suicide involving a firearm. A research study by the Children's Hospital of Philadelphia found that 23,649 Americans ages nineteen or younger died from gunshots, and the rates in rural communities were similar to those in urban areas. Rural regions reported 4 deaths per 100,000 children and teens, and urban communities reported 4.6 per 100,000. While the death rates were about the same, the researchers did find differences in the types of gun death that were prevalent in these areas. Children and teens in urban communities were more likely to be the victims of gun homicide, while those in rural communities experienced higher rates of gun suicide and accidental death.

Myths & FACTS

Myth: Gun violence is at an all-time high.

Fact: According to a 2014 survey by the Pew Research Center, 56 percent of Americans believe gun crime is higher than it was twenty years ago, while only 12 percent think it is lower. In fact, gun violence has been in a steady decline since the 1990s. The number of Americans killed by guns was 49 percent lower in 2010 than it was in 1993. There has also been a decrease in the number of violent crimes committed with the help of a gun. In 2011, the prevalence of such crimes was 75 percent lower than it was in 1993. However, mass shootings have been happening more frequently since the mid-2000s, according to Politico, and they have become deadlier because guns are becoming more powerful.

Myth: Having a gun will protect you from gun violence.

Fact: Gun owners are no more likely than those who don't own guns to protect themselves from a violent attack, but they are more likely to die in a firearm-related incident.

According to the Pew Research Center, 67 percent of Americans who own a gun do so because they want to protect themselves. However, a 2017 study by the National Bureau of Economic Research debunks the myth that guns make people safer by illustrating that states where "right to carry" laws were passed saw an up-tick in gun violence. In other words, the more people that own guns, the more gun-related crimes there are.

Myth: Guns don't kill people. People kill people.

Fact: This slogan was popularized by the National Rifle Association (NRA) and is popular with gun rights advocates. It asserts that the real problem with guns is not the weapon itself, but the weapon in the hands of the wrong person. In truth, access to guns drastically increases one's chances of death or gun-related injury.

CHAPTER THREE

Gun Violence in the News

Sadly, gun violence is so commonplace in the United States that it often doesn't make news headlines. However, there are some types of gun violence that are widely reported in the media. These include mass shootings and incidences of police shooting unarmed black men.

Mass Shootings

The biggest conversations about gun violence and gun control are usually sparked by mass shootings. A mass shooting is defined as any gun-related incident in which a single shooter kills more than four people. It does not include gang-related shootings or shootings that happen as the result of another serious crime, like a robbery. In the United States, there are more mass shootings than in any other developed nation in the world. Though mass shootings make up a small percentage of

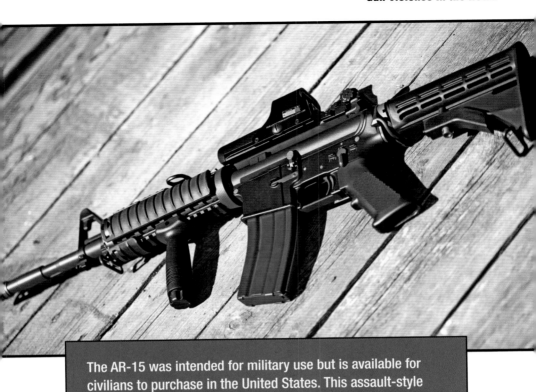

The AR-15 was intended for military use but is available for civilians to purchase in the United States. This assault-style weapon is often used during mass shootings.

all gun-related deaths and injuries, the large number of casualties tied to a single incident often leaves the public in shock.

The horrible impact of mass shootings is especially exacerbated by civilian access to high-powered assault-style weapons like the AR-15. According to the *New York Times*, 157 people have been killed on American soil in mass shootings where this weapon was used. The military-grade weapon has been used in mass shootings across the country, in Newtown, Connecticut, Las Vegas, Nevada, San Bernardino,

In the Mandalay Bay hotel in Las Vegas, Nevada, a gunman opened fire on concert-goers and killed forty-nine people on October 1, 2017.

California, and Parkland, Florida. Many experts refer to the AR-15 as the mass shooter's weapon of choice. It is no surprise that a person who wants to inflict maximum damage and wreak the most havoc would choose to do so with a gun that was once used only by the military. The AR-15's bullets travel at three times the speed of light and were designed to be incredibly deadly. Upon hitting a target, the bullet bursts into tiny parts, causing destruction and ravaging victims' bodies.

Nevertheless, semiautomatic weapons, such as the AR-15, are marketed to everyday civilians, and they have become one of the most popular guns to own. According to an estimate by the National Shooting Sports Federation, the AR-15 is the gun of choice in one out of five gun purchases by Americans.

Mass shootings are typically followed by a few days or weeks of public outrage and demand for tighter gun-control laws. However, despite calls for the government to pass laws to keep powerful guns like the AR-15 off the streets, these guns are still available for civilian purchase.

Case Study: Australia Gives Hope for Successful Intervention

The Port Arthur massacre occurred in Tasmania, Australia, on April 28, 1996, at a popular tourist site in the southeastern part of the country. Martin Bryant, a twenty-eight-year-old man from a nearby suburb, opened fire on a crowd with a semiautomatic rifle, taking thirty-five lives and wounding twenty-three people. Because he used such a powerful weapon, it took less than a minute for Bryant to kill his first twelve victims. He was captured by the police after a long standoff and eventually received thirty-five life sentences for the gruesome murders.

This tragedy was the largest mass shooting in Australia. In response, the country's then-prime minister, John Howard, introduced strict gun-control laws called the National Firearms Agreement. The laws banned certain semiautomatic, self-loading rifles and shotguns, and imposed stricter licensing and registration requirements for those who wanted to purchase firearms. To rid the country of the deadly, banned weapons, Australia's prime minister also implemented a mandatory buyback program.

It is estimated that Australians sold 640,000 firearms back to the government and surrendered 60,000 guns banned by the new laws. More than 700,000 weapons left the streets of Australia, ultimately creating a safer country. A study by the Harvard Injury Control Research Center estimated a nearly 20 percent decrease in Australia's civilian gun ownership after these measures were taken. In 2002, Australia implemented even more extensive gun laws, restricting the caliber, barrel length, and capacity for sports handguns.

The Australian government's intervention after this tragedy has saved many lives. Before the NFA was enacted, there were thirteen mass shootings in Australia in which four or more people died at one time. After the introduction of the stricter gun laws, that number fell to zero. Australia has yet to experience another mass shooting.

These gun laws also impacted the country's homicide and suicide rates. In the seven years before the NFA (1989 to 1995), the average annual firearm suicide death rate was 2.6 for every 100,000 citizens. Seven years after the government-sanctioned buyback program was fully implemented, the number of suicides was reduced by more than half, according to FactCheck.org. The homicide rate also fell from 0.43 per 100,000 to 0.25. Studies have found these drops to be directly linked to the legislation because the largest decreases in firearm-related deaths were seen in states with higher buyback rates, compared to states where rates were lower.

Mass Shooting at Sandy Hook Elementary School

What started as an ordinary day for kids and teachers at Sandy Hook Elementary School in Newtown, Connecticut, ended in tragedy on December 14, 2012. After killing his mother in their home, twenty-year-old Adam Lanza armed himself with three guns from the

A memorial created for the victims of the Sandy Hook Elementary School massacre, where twenty children between six and seven years old were killed in 2012.

house—a semiautomatic AR-15 assault rifle and two pistols—and put on black military-style pants and a military vest. He then drove to a nearby elementary school and fatally shot twenty children between the ages of six and seven, as well as six adult faculty members. Before he was apprehended by police, Lanza turned the gun on himself and committed suicide.

The Sandy Hook Elementary School massacre was the deadliest mass shooting to occur in a grade school or high school in the United States. It was also the fourth-deadliest mass shooting. As the images of the children and teachers who lost their lives that day began to circulate in the media, public outcry and outrage prompted renewed debate about gun control across the nation. Gun-control advocates proposed a universal background-check system and called for a ban of all semiautomatic weapons and magazines capable of holding more than ten rounds of ammunition. However, despite the support of a number of politicians, attempts to introduce legislation to curtail access to semiautomatic guns were defeated and never became federal law.

The Heroes Who Save Lives When Gun Violence Erupts

Victoria Leigh Soto was a twenty-seven-year-old teacher at Sandy Hook Elementary School when Adam Lanza entered the school armed with several guns. After shooting and killing fifteen students and the teacher in the first classroom, Lanza made his way over to the neighboring class. He found Soto, who had just finished hiding several children in a closet. She tried to distract Lanza by telling him there were no kids in the room because they were all in the gym. Sadly, however, a few of the kids got scared and tried to run out of the closet toward safety. The gunman opened fire on the children. Soto threw her body in the line of fire to try to shield them from the spray of bullets and was tragically killed.

In honor of Victoria Leigh Soto's heroic attempt to save the lives of her students, Soto's alma mater, Eastern Connecticut State University,

President Barack Obama presents Victoria Soto's family, Donna and Carlos Soto Sr., with the 2012 Presidential Citizens Medal.

established the Victoria Leigh Soto Endowed Memorial Scholarship Fund, which is awarded to students pursuing a degree in teaching. Soto was also posthumously awarded the Presidential Citizens Medal by Barack Obama. The medal is the government's second-highest civilian award given to Americans who perform "exemplary deeds of service" for their country.

Safety Guide for Surviving a Mass Shooting

Though rare, mass shootings can happen anywhere. There have been reports of gunmen firing on crowds of people in malls, schools, movie theaters, concerts, tourist destinations, and grocery stores. In truth, no place is completely safe from the potential eruption of gun violence, so it is important to always take precautions. The University of Wisconsin's Police Department released a guide to the public with advice on what to do in the event that there is an active shooter.

Always be aware of your environment. Every time you walk into a building, take note of the exits. In case of an emergency, you will know which direction to go to safely escape danger. Also, be aware of the people in your environment. Does anyone look suspicious? Can you see any weapons in plain view? Are there security guards or police officers nearby? While it is not good to be paranoid, taking quick notes of your environment when you first enter can make a world of difference if violence should happen to erupt.

Don't just stand there: run and hide! When in danger, our bodies often naturally respond by going into flight or fight mode, but sometimes fear can be paralyzing. Never stand motionless in the event of a shooting. This will make you an easy target. Your first response should be to run away from the sound of chaos (screaming, shooting, or stomping feet) toward an exit or trained personnel. If an exit is not an option, look for a safe place to hide but remain on guard. Whatever you do, never come out of a hiding place without knowing that the coast is completely clear. This could jeopardize your safety and the safety of anyone else who may be hiding with you.

Fight only when you must. No one wants to have to confront an armed gunman, but sometimes fighting is the only option.

Call for help and try to help others only when it is safe to do so. When you are certain that all shooting has ceased and the violence has ended, immediately call emergency services. Do not stop to do so in the midst of running away from danger or looking for safety. Doing so may distract you from making your escape or alert the shooter to your whereabouts.

Why Black Lives Matter Matters

Guns in the hands of people who are racially biased or harbor negative feelings about a group of people can be extremely dangerous. Videos and images of black men, women, and children being shot and killed by police officers are frequently played on the evening news and often go viral on social media. These killings receive attention for good reason. Despite comprising 13 percent

Black Lives Matters founders Alicia Garza (*center*) and Opal Tometi (*right*) speak onstage with Patrice Cullors (*left*) during The New York Women's Foundation Celebrating Women Breakfast in 2015.

of the American population, black people account for about 25 percent of those who are killed by police every year. Mappingpoliceviolence.org reports that black people are three times more likely to be shot and killed by police compared to their white counterparts. In such police shooting deaths, 30 percent of black victims are unarmed. The 2014 statistics compiled by the website revealed that fewer than one in three of the black people shot by police were suspected of a serious violent crime or allegedly armed.

While these statistics alone are very disheartening, the fact that police are rarely held accountable for these killings is even more tragic. Less than 1 percent of police shootings and killings result in officers being convicted of a crime. For the black community, the continued lack of accountability feels like an egregious miscarriage of justice. How can black people believe in a justice system that does not believe that black lives matter?

The Death of Trayvon Martin and the Birth of a Movement

On the night of February 26, 2012, seventeen-year-old Trayvon Martin was walking home from a local convenience store, wearing a hoodie and carrying a packet of candy, when he was intercepted by a man named George Zimmerman. Due to a string of recent crimes in the gated community, Zimmerman was appointed the head of the self-organized neighborhood watch, tasked with keeping an eye out for possible criminals. Within moments of their interaction, George Zimmerman pulled out his gun, fired a single shot, and killed Trayvon Martin. Zimmerman had been licensed to carry a firearm.

Though Zimmerman was initially arrested, he was released from jail within five hours.

Protesters hold signs with Trayvon Martin's photo, demanding justice for the seventeen-year-old boy's death after he was gunned down by George Zimmerman in 2012.

53

Pictures released of Zimmerman on the night of the incident showed he had a bloody nose and lacerations on his head and face. Based on this evidence, the Sanford police chief said Zimmerman acted in self-defense and Florida's Stand Your Ground law allows for the use of lethal force to defend oneself in the event of imminent danger.

Outrage about this shooting and the police department's response spread across the nation. Protests were staged and a petition calling for Zimmerman's arrest accrued 2.2 million signatures. Amid this public outrage, police charged Zimmerman with second-degree murder, but in the end, he was acquitted of the crime.

In response to Trayvon Martin's tragic murder and the acquittal of George Zimmerman, the Black Lives Matter movement was formed by Alicia Garza, Patrisse Cullors, and Opal Tometi to raise awareness of issues of racism, racial profiling, police violence, and bias within the criminal justice system. The movement became nationally recognized for its large-scale protests and the popularization of the hashtag #BlackLivesMatter.

As a result, since 2014, there has been a significant increase in news coverage involving police shootings and black victims. The public has become more aware of the fact that unarmed victims killed by police are more likely to be minorities. This awareness has led to the implementation of several efforts to curtail police violence against minorities, including a push for legislation to ensure police wear body cameras, police training on racial bias, and proposals to ensure police interaction with civilians does not escalate. While some of these measures have been adopted across the nation, black people still face disproportionate profiling and violence by police officers.

The Charleston Church Shooting

Dylann Storm Roof walked into Emanuel African Episcopal church in Charleston, South Carolina, in the middle of a service on June 17, 2015. The church's members—a pastor, an elderly minister, eight women, one young man, and a little girl—were just about to close their eyes and bow their heads to begin a prayer when gunshots erupted. Roof opened fire on the small church gathering with a Glock handgun. Nine people were killed and one person was injured. All of the victims of the shooting were African American, and it soon became clear that Dylan Roof had planned it that way.

After a long manhunt, Roof was caught by police the next morning. He not only admitted to his crime, but clearly stated the motivation for the horrific act.

This memorial was created by the community to honor the victims of the Charleston Church shooting, in which a white supremacist killed nine churchgoers.

Dylann Storm Roof was a racist white supremacist who hoped his actions would ignite a race war. He also reportedly told investigators that he almost did not go through with the shooting because the black members of the church were so welcoming and treated him respectfully. A few days after the shooting, a website owned by Roof was discovered. It contained photos of Roof posing with symbols typically worn by white supremacists and Nazis as well as a manifesto that spelled out his racist views toward black people and other minority groups. Roof wrote:

> I have no choice. I am not in the position to, alone, go into the ghetto and fight. I chose Charleston because it is most [sic] historic city in my state, and at one time had the highest ratio of blacks to Whites in the country. We have no

skinheads, no real KKK, no one doing anything but talking on the internet. Well someone has to have the bravery to take it to the real world, and I guess that has to be me.

Dylann Storm Roof's actions shined a light on the ongoing racial tensions in the United States. It also forced the nation to acknowledge the role of white men in domestic terrorism and the vital role guns play in their ability to commit atrocious acts of mass violence.

CHAPTER FOUR

Coping with Trauma and Loss

I t is never easy to lose a close friend or loved one and it is especially difficult to cope when that loss is the result of violent crime. Gun violence is traumatic and those who survive incidents involving firearms can be scarred both physically and emotionally. These scars take time to heal, and sometimes it can help to be aware of what that healing process could look like.

Common Reactions to Trauma

People suffering from trauma can experience an entire range of physical, emotional, and mental reactions to trauma. Trauma can impact a person's physical well-being by resulting in fatigue or

It is normal to have a range of physical and emotional reactions after experiencing a traumatic event or losing a loved one.

exhaustion. It is often linked to disturbed sleep, and many report having sleep troubles and being unable to fall asleep or stay asleep after a traumatic experience. Other physical responses can include nausea, vomiting, dizziness, headaches, excessive sweating, and increased heart rate.

On an emotional level, trauma is very disruptive. In the immediate aftermath of a traumatic event, it is common to experience fear, anxiety, panic, and shock— difficulty believing what has happened and feeling confused or detached from the situation. It is very common to feel numb and withdraw from others, including close friends and family members. Trauma survivors sometimes still feel like danger is lurking or like the traumatic event is still unfolding, resulting in jumpiness or being very easy to startle.

In many cases, behavioral changes also become apparent. Those exposed to trauma will often do anything to avoid reminders of the event, or they may become unhealthily preoccupied with thinking about the traumatic experience. They may also become hyperfocused on recovery-related tasks and lose touch with normal daily routines. To help cope with the emotional, physical, and behavioral reactions to trauma, some may turn to substances like alcohol, drugs, or cigarettes.

In the aftermath of traumatic violent incidents, it is not uncommon for the body to go through a "let down" period. In the midst of a high-stress moment, the body responds by releasing a number of hormones that help the person cope in the moment but have detrimental effects afterward. As a result, a person's immune responses can be compromised, resulting in increased likelihood of becoming sick. Other "let down" responses include depression, avoidance, guilt, oversensitivity, and withdrawal. It is important to recognize that such emotions and reactions are not permanent—in most cases, they subside as the body and mind heals. For some, the feelings can be persistent and overwhelming. In such instances, it is best to seek help from a health care professional, a therapist, or a school counselor.

Grieving: The Road to Healing

Loss is an inevitable part of life, and it is also extremely hard to deal with. The grieving process helps people work through the pain, come to terms with loss, and move on in a healthy way. Everyone has a different grieving process and there is no set time limit for grieving. It can sometimes take months and even years to fully recover from loss or trauma. There are steps to every process, including grieving. Being aware of these steps can sometimes help.

Acknowledge that it hurts. Denying your emotions won't make them go away. The process of grieving begins with letting yourself feel the way you really feel, even if your emotions include anger and other feelings that make you feel confused.

Recognize that grief may cause emotional triggers. Emotions or powerful memories of the person you lost may hit you unexpectedly and make it hard for you to focus on what you're doing. This is a normal part of the grieving process.

Remember that your grieving process may not look like anyone else's. Don't let anyone tell you how you should be grieving or how long the grieving process should take.

Reach out to your support network. Finding a friend, teacher, counselor, or someone who can listen to you without judging you and without telling you what to think can make a world of difference. You may also consider joining a support group for people suffering from grief and loss.

Know the difference between depression and grieving. It's normal to feel sad after losing a loved

It's always a good idea to share your feelings with someone who can listen in a nonjudgmental way. This could be a trained therapist, counselor, or a trusted friend.

one, but if you feel you are becoming depressed, it's important to seek help from a medical professional. Signs of depression can include having trouble maintaining your normal routine (for instance, going to school and keeping up with school work), self-harming, and feeling like life is not worth living.

Take a Break from the News

News reports of gun violence can leave people feeling saddened and fearful, even if they didn't personally know the victims. Whether you are exposed to gun violence through personal experience or the media, you may find yourself stressed out or anxious. It's important to pay attention to these feelings and to take time to nurture your mental and emotional health by practicing self-care. Self-care includes daily practices like eating well, getting enough sleep, exercising, and taking the time to acknowledge and understand difficult emotions. It also involves knowing when to take a break from the news.

When tragedy strikes, the news media is an immediate source of information for people across the world. Through hearing first-person accounts of the incident, people who never knew the victims may feel a connection to those who experienced the tragedy. Tales of heroism, pain, loss, and perseverance help people to feel empathy for victims and perhaps also inspire people across the nation to take action. Though this sense of connection through the news and media can be positive and can increase community awareness and involvement, repeated exposure to reports of tragedy can be a source of stress and anxiety.

After the 1995 Oklahoma City bombings, researchers found a correlation between adolescent

SKY 10 LIVE

BREAKING NEWS
Multiple Shooting Victims At
Fort Laud.-Hollywood Int'l Airpo

Research shows that watching too much news coverage of violent events can cause PTSD. Sometimes it's necessary to switch off the television or step away from social media.

exposure to media coverage of the attack and increased anxiety. According to a study published in the *Annals of Clinical Psychiatry*, eighty-eight sixth-grade students from a middle school in a community 100 miles (160 kilometers) away from Oklahoma City were surveyed and many reported exposure to bomb-related media. This exposure proved to be traumatic for some. Researchers found that children who spent

much of their time paying attention to news coverage of the bombings reported more traumalike symptoms. The study also found that students who were exposed to print media were more likely to have enduring posttraumatic stress connected to the bombing compared to those exposed to broadcast coverage. The results suggest that children may have lingering reactions to highly publicized traumatic incidents.

While it is good to be informed, sometimes it is crucial to switch off the television and take a break from the news. Repeated exposure to violent news coverage can be retraumatizing.

Gun Violence in Video Games

Most young people play video games, many of which have violent themes and can include gun violence. For example, in *Grand Theft Auto*, one of the best-selling games worldwide, gamers play a character who often encounters violent situations,

uses a gun, and steals cars. Oftentimes, when violence explodes in a community or school, violent gaming is cited as a cause. There has been ongoing debate and plenty of research to try to untangle the real-world consequences of teen access to violent games. Based on this growing body of information, most researchers have reached the same conclusion: there is no evidence to establish a definitive link between violent gaming and real-world violence.

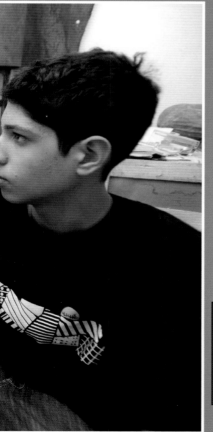

The government, researchers who study gun crime, and even the American Psychological Association (APA) have all taken a public stance against linking gun violence to gaming violence. When California tried to enforce a law to restrict the sale of violent games to minors, the gaming industry pushed back by taking the state to federal court. In 2011, the US

(continued on the next page)

Although many people believe that violent video games lead to violent behavior in real life, there is no scientific evidence linking the two.

(continued from the previous page)

Supreme Court ruled that research did not find a clear connection between violent video games and aggressive behavior and reiterated the position that games—like other forms of media—are protected by the First Amendment.

In 2017, the Media Psychology and Technology division of the APA released a statement suggesting that reporters and policy makers cease linking mass shootings to violent media, given the lack of evidence for a connection. It read, "Journalists and policy makers do their constituencies a disservice in cases where they link acts of real-world violence with the perpetrators' exposure to violent video games or other violent media. There's little scientific evidence to support the connection, and it may distract us from addressing those issues that we know contribute to real-world violence."

A Simple Beginner's Meditation

Meditation creates a sacred time to relax and reenergize the mind, body, and soul. The benefits of meditation include stress reduction, increased self-awareness, and improved concentration, and many people report increased feelings of happiness and a willingness to be more accepting and open. The practice is also known to have incredible physical benefits, including decreasing blood pressure and boosting immune health. Adding a simple meditation to a daily routine can help anyone persevere through emotionally and physically stressful moments.

Designate your safe meditation space. This place can be in a bedroom, outdoors, or anywhere that is quiet. Return to the same place every day for your meditation to create a sense of consistency and safety.

Begin with a few stretches. The body tends to hold a lot of tension, especially when a person is trying to heal from trauma. Release this tension from the body by dedicating a few moments to stretching before beginning a meditation.

Sit straight and allow your body to relax. When seated straight, the body's weight is evenly distributed. The force of gravity acts as a support and keeps your body aligned. A straight-seated position is not completely erect—there is a small curve to the spine. If you are unable to get comfortable while trying to sit straight on a floor, start in a chair that provides back support.

Let your thoughts wander. For the first few minutes of a meditation, the mind will wander and be flooded with thoughts and reflections. That is OK. Eventually your thoughts will settle down.

Practicing meditation can reduce stress, improve focus, and help you to cope with some of the symptoms of PTSD and grief.

Breathe deeply, paying close attention to each breath. Inhale through the nose and exhale through the mouth. Each inhale should fill the lungs, forcing the tummy to extend outward. If your mind wanders, return your focus back to your breath.

Maintain this meditation practice for two to three minutes to start. Meditation is beneficial even if you do it for only a minute a day. Any amount of time dedicated to the practice is time well spent.

10 Great Questions to Ask a Grief Counselor

1. I'm having a hard time concentrating in school because I keep thinking about this traumatic event. What can I do?

2. Can you help me identify all of my feelings surrounding this trauma?

3. Will I always feel this way?

4. How do I know if I am depressed or just grieving?

5. Will medication help me?

6. How can I track my healing progress?

7. Am I the only one experiencing these feelings?

8. How can I support others experiencing trauma?

9. Are there any resources that I can access to help me through this difficult time?

10. Can you recommend a support group for survivors of violence?

The Road Toward Ending Gun Violence

n her 2014 memoir *A Fighting Chance*, US senator Elizabeth Warren made the following observation:

> We lose eight children and teenagers to gun violence every day. If a mysterious virus suddenly started killing eight of our children every day, America would mobilize teams of doctors and public health officials. We would move heaven and earth until we found a way to protect our children. But not with gun violence.

The United States has a serious gun violence problem. It is hard to turn a blind eye to the horrifying reality these weapons create. It can be seen in the bloody streets of Chicago and all

Senator Elizabeth Warren walks with Parkland students during the March for Our Lives rally in Boston on March 24, 2018.

over the evening news as details of another mass shooting spree unfold. It can be seen in the pained faces of parents, friends, and teachers who are forced to bury their loved ones because a gun stole their lives. And yet, many politicians and citizens alike remain staunchly against gun-control laws that could protect Americans from enduring the pain caused by firearms.

Though progun activists cite their Second Amendment right to bear arms, it is also every American's right to be safe from gun violence. Every time a firearm is used to harm a citizen, that right is infringed upon. The ubiquity of guns in the country, as well as the accessibility of high-powered, semiautomatic weapons, poses serious safety risks for all. Writer and commentator DaShanne Stokes said, "Violence isn't a Democrat or Republican problem. It's an American problem, requiring an American solution." Everyone can do something to help make their own communities safer places.

The NRA: Protector of American Rights or Gun Industry Puppet?

The National Rifle Association (NRA) is a gun rights organization with a membership that surpassed five million in May 2013 and continues to grow annually. Founded in 1871, the group was first organized to protect the Second Amendment right to bear arms and also advance shooting and hunting as sports. However, over the centuries, the NRA has become one of the top three most influential lobbying organizations in the nation. While the organization prides itself on being free of any political ties, much of its funding comes directly from the gun-manufacturing industry. According to the organization's 2010 IRS form, the NRA made $20.9 million (about 10 percent of its revenue) from selling ads to gun manufacturers and marketing its products. According to Business Insider, between 2005

Marjory Stoneman Douglas High School student Emma González delivers a speech at the March for Our Lives rally in Boston on March 24, 2018.

and 2013, the gun industry and its corporate allies donated between $20 million and $52.6 million to the NRA, creating a problematic bond between America's most influential gun organization and the people who manufacture weapons.

According to a report published by the Violence Policy Center, "Today's NRA is a virtual subsidiary of the gun industry.... While the NRA portrays itself as protecting the 'freedom' of individual gun owners, it's actually working to protect the freedom of the gun industry to manufacture and sell virtually any weapon or accessory."

This spells trouble for Americans and policy makers who are interested in implementing gun-control laws to curtail access to dangerous firearms. The power of the NRA and the funding it receives from the gun industry stifles many attempts at federal intervention to stop gun violence. When President Barack Obama introduced proposals—including restarting federal research on gun violence and calling on Congress to pass an extensive package of legislative proposals, like universal background checks and a ban on assault weapons and high-capacity magazines—to curtail gun violence after the Sandy Hook massacre, his proposals were swiftly defeated. The only rule that survived required the Social Security Administration to report disability-benefit recipients with mental health conditions to the FBI's background check system, which is used to screen firearm buyers. This background check law was rescinded by President Donald Trump in February 2017. The NRA had spent $30 million in support of Trump's 2016 presidential campaign, according to the Center for Responsive Politics.

How to Protect Yourself from Gun Violence

Many young people experience gun violence in their own communities. Family members or friends may own guns, increasing the chances of a dangerous encounter with a firearm. Peers may bring the deadly weapons to school to show off. It is important to navigate these situations and to know that there are many things you can do to keep yourself safe from gun violence.

- **Don't be afraid to report anyone who looks suspicious or potentially dangerous.** Homeland Security warns, "If you see something, say something," and that very much applies to suspicious or potentially dangerous situations with firearms. Whether a gun is left in easy

(continued on the next page)

(continued from the previous page)

reach or being carried by a suspicious-looking person, do not be afraid to alert an adult.

- **Stay away from loaded or unloaded guns.** Many accidents happen while playing with firearms. Whether or not you believe a gun is loaded, guns are not toys and should never be treated as such.
- **Report anyone underage who owns or possesses a firearm or ammunition.** Under federal law, the minimum age to purchase and possess a firearm is eighteen, and in some instances (like when purchasing a firearm from a licensed dealer), the minimum age is twenty-one.
- **Steer clear of gangs.** When trying to bolster their numbers, gangs frequently target young people for recruitment. Being affiliated with a gang puts you at much greater risk of exposure to gun violence.
- **Stay away from street fights.** In a split second, a simple street fight can end in the eruption of a gunfight.
- **Stay away from drugs and drug dealers.** The single most powerful predictor of violence is drug abuse. Many studies have concluded that using drugs and selling drugs puts people at an elevated risk for violence, according to American Addiction Centers.

Gun Buyback Programs

Many states across the nation have implemented gun buyback programs to get more guns out of the hands of civilians and off of the streets. The programs offer a safe space for gun owners to sell their guns without fear of persecution from the government. Typically, police officers act as liaisons between the community and the government by purchasing firearms from residents in the community and then handing them over to federal bodies. However, research has proven that these programs do little to lower rates of gun violence. Oftentimes, participants in the programs are not the people who are likely to act violently with firearms, and many of the weapons recovered tend to be old and barely functional. For example, a buyback in Tucson, Arizona, in 2013 collected about two hundred firearms and gave away thousands of dollars worth of grocery store gift cards, but many of the firearms were old and didn't work. "Every gun that came in was an old gun, no assault weapons," Tom Ditsch, who watched the event, told the Associated Press. "They didn't even take any weapons off the streets." While buyback programs are not necessarily successful in curbing gun violence, they do raise awareness about America's gun problem, which is important in itself.

The Parkland Shooting and the Fight for Gun Control

After a mass school shooting at Marjory Stoneman Douglas High School in Parkland, Florida, on February 14, 2018, the student survivors of the shooting sparked a national movement when they spoke out publicly about the need for increased gun control. At a gun-control rally just a few days after the shooting, seventeen-year-old Emma González, who survived the Parkland shooting, said, "Every single person up here today, all these people should be home grieving. But instead we are up here standing together because if all our government and president can do is send thoughts and prayers, then it's time for victims to be the change that we need to see."

The Parkland survivors continued to speak out and organize for the need for commonsense gun laws. One month after the shooting,

Survivors of the shooting at Marjory Stoneman Douglas High School spoke with elected officials to voice their demand for tighter gun control measures.

thousands of high school students across the country organized a walkout to bring attention to the need for gun control, and dozens more descended on the White House in Washington, DC, to bring their message to the politicians who have the power to change the laws. On March 24, 2018, hundreds of thousands of people came together for the March for Our Lives, a student-led protest demanding gun control, and the Parkland students led a gun-control rally in Washington, DC, that drew a crowd of close to eight hundred thousand people, according to most estimates.

In response to the bravery displayed by Parkland's students, various companies stopped selling semiautomatic weapons, pulled support for the NRA, and changed their policies around gun sales. Dick's Sporting Goods, the largest sporting retailer in the nation, stopped selling semiautomatic weapons like the one used in the Parkland shooting and also raised its minimum age to purchase a gun to twenty-one. "As we sat and talked about it with our management team, it was—to a person—that this is what we

According to most estimates, the March for Our Lives rally in Washington, DC, on March 24, 2018, attracted almost eight thousand people in support of gun control.

need to do," Dick's CEO Edward Stack said about the decision. "These kids talk about enough is enough. We concluded if these kids are brave enough to organize and do what they're doing, we should be brave enough to take this stand." Walmart and Kroger's (which sells guns at its Fred Meyer brand stores) followed suit.

Eight days after the shooting and subsequent protests, First National Bank of Omaha became the first company to pull support from the NRA. It scrapped giving special incentives, special rates, and discounts to the association's members. Delta and United Airlines followed suit, as did car rental companies Hertz, Avis, and Alamo, and insurance companies MetLife and Chubb.

The Parkland shooting also shifted public opinion in support of stricter gun laws. According to a 2018 Politico/Morning Consult poll, 68 percent of Americans believed stricter gun laws should be enforced nationwide. While it is common for spikes in gun support to occur right after mass shootings, that number represents the largest growth in support for stricter gun laws since the poll's inception. After the Pulse nightclub shooting in 2016, only 58 percent of Americans supported stricter gun laws, and following the mass shooting that claimed fifty-eight lives in Las Vegas in 2017, 64 percent did.

This underscores not only changes in the way Americans view their relationship to guns, but also the power of passionate young people. The words and actions of these brave teens forced major corporations to reconsider their affiliations and choose public safety over profit. Young people can also wield this power in the voting booth to help decide which elected officials remain in power and which are voted out.

Speak Up if You See or Hear Something

Angela McDevitt, a seventeen-year-old girl from New York, made the tough decision to turn in a friend who she thought might be plotting an attack on a school—and that decision may have saved many lives. McDevitt secretly tipped police off after her eighteen-year-old friend Jack Sawyer sent her a series of disturbing messages. Sawyer allegedly wrote that he intended to carry out a mass shooting at his former high school in Fair Haven, Vermont.

McDevitt told police that it was very hard for her to turn in her friend, whom she met at a mental health treatment center. Police arrested Jack Sawyer and

(continued on the next page)

(continued from the previous page)

found a journal he had been keeping, titled "Journal of an active shooter." It detailed plans of the attack and also led authorities to recover a shotgun and ammunition the teen had recently purchased. Republican governor Phil Scott praised the bravery of McDevitt, saying, "It was only by the grace of God and the courage of a young woman who spoke up that we averted a horrific outcome."

The courage of a single person can make a world of difference when it comes to averting potentially dangerous situations. There are anonymous hotlines where anyone can submit a tip with information that a friend, family member, or even acquaintance has plans to use a gun in a crime. That includes crime on any scale. Every violent act committed with a gun has the potential to end or ruin a life.

Government Response to the Fight for Gun Control

Despite the outcry, protests, shift in public opinion, and corporate action that has happened as a result of mass shootings, the government has done little to create meaningful legislation to curb access to guns. When

Parkland students and parents asked for more gun-control laws, President Donald Trump responded by trying to bring more guns into schools. During the press conference with teachers and students, Trump argued that Aaron Feis, a football coach at Marjory Stoneman Douglas High School who used his body to shield students and lost his life, would still be alive had he been armed.

Trump said:

> But if he had a firearm, he wouldn't have had to run, he would have shot him, and that would have been the end of it. This would only obviously be for people who are very adept at handling a gun. It's called concealed carry, where a teacher would have a concealed gun on them. They'd go for special training and they would be there and you would no longer have a gun-free zone. Gun-free zone to a maniac, because they're all cowards, a gun-free zone is: "Let's go in and let's attack, because bullets aren't coming back at us."

Gun-control advocates were outraged by the president's proposed solutions. Why would he suggest putting more guns in schools, when studies have long proved that guns increase the likelihood that someone will be accidentally hurt? Why did he not consider parent and student suggestions to strengthen gun laws?

Like many politicians, Donald Trump may not want to challenge the current gun law status quo because lax

President Donald Trump addressed Marjory Stoneman Douglas High School students and their families and suggested arming teachers to prevent future school shootings.

gun-control laws generate millions of dollars in revenue for organizations like the NRA, who in turn fund politicians. The NRA has, for decades, donated to political candidates and paid for expensive lobbyists to influence elected officials. According to the Center for Responsive Politics, "NRA support for some members of the 115th Congress now reaches well into the seven-figure range." The organization also spent more than $30 million supporting Donald Trump's presidential campaign.

Elected officials are not always invested in the best interests of the American people, but by paying close attention to local and national politics and going out to vote, young people can hold politicians accountable. Stoneman Douglas senior Delaney Tarr told reporters during a rally:

> We've spoke to only a few legislators, and, try as they might, the most we've gotten out of them is "We'll keep you in our thoughts. You are so strong. You are so

Delaney Tarr, a senior at Marjory Stoneman Douglas High School, told politicians that she and her fellow survivors were tired of "thoughts and prayers" and wanted real action.

powerful." We know what we want. We want gun reform. We want commonsense gun laws. ... We want change . . . We've had enough of thoughts and prayers. If you supported us, you would have made a change long ago. So this is to every lawmaker out there: No longer can you take money from the NRA. We are coming after you. We are coming after every single one of you, demanding that you take action.

Hope for the Future?

Gun violence impacts everyone in the United States: black families plagued by gang-related gun violence in inner cities; children and teachers in the nation's schools, who only want a safe place to learn and teach; the mentally ill who, in times of desperation, may turn to firearms to end their lives; mothers, daughters, fathers, sons, and everyone else experiencing the fear, grief, and pain caused by gun violence.

Though gun-control advocates have been demanding commonsense gun laws for decades with little in the way of meaningful response from elected officials, the momentum generated by grassroots movements such as Black Lives Matter and the March for Our Lives illustrate the power of people coming together from all walks of life to stand up and make their voices heard. Examples of successful gun-control measures in countries such as Australia prove that it's possible to curtail gun violence. Together, Americans can effect change to make the country safer for everyone.

accidental gun-related death Any death involving a gun that is unintentional.

criminal background check The process of gathering information about a person's criminal history based on criminal records.

discrimination The mistreatment of people because of their race, gender, religion, sexual orientation, beliefs, or another aspect of their identity.

disenfranchised Deprived of rights or power.

empowerment The process of becoming stronger in one's own convictions and fighting to reclaim one's own rights.

grieving The process of mourning after a loss.

gun buyback program A program created by local law enforcement or the government to get guns off of the streets by offering citizens money if they turn in their firearms.

gun-free zone School zones, where guns are restricted by federal law.

gun laws Laws that regulate civilian access to guns.

gun manufacturing The production and creation of firearms.

gun rights According to the Second Amendment, every American citizen has the right to bear arms (own a gun).

gun violence Any violence committed with the use of a firearm.

homicide A violent act in which someone takes the life of another; murder.

meditation The practice of working toward inner peace by focusing inward and working on breathing exercises and relaxation.

redlining Racially discriminatory banking practices that limit the access of people of color to mortgages in primarily white neighborhoods.

rural area An area that is sparsely populated, rather than a large town or city.

segregation The separation of people based on race.

self-care An act of self-love that increases emotional, physical, and psychological well-being.

semiautomatic firearm A gun with self-loading ability that can inflict massive casualties.

traumatic event An incident that causes physical, psychological, or emotional pain.

ubiquitous Found in many places or everywhere.

urban area A large city or metropolis where many people live.

Brady Campaign to Prevent Gun Violence
840 First Street NE, Suite 400
Washington, DC 20002
(202) 370-8100
Website: http://www.bradycampaign.org
Facebook: @BradyCampaign
Twitter: @BradyBuzz
The Brady Campaign is an organization dedicated to reducing gun violence in the United States. It focuses on policy changes to keep guns out of the wrong hands.

Coalition for Gun Control
PO Box 90062
1488 Queen Street West
Toronto, ON M6K 3K3
Canada
(416) 604-0209
Website: http://guncontrol.ca
Twitter: @CGCGuncontrol
The Coalition for Gun Control was founded in Montreal, Canada, in the wake of a tragic mass shooting in the city. The organization promotes policy changes to restrict certain high-powered firearms and advocates for public education about safe gun storage.

Coalition to Stop Gun Violence
805 15th Street NW
Washington, DC 20005
(202) 408-0061
Website: https://www.csgv.org
Facebook: @CoalitiontoStopGunViolence
Twitter: @CSGV
The Coalition to Stop Gun Violence is a nonprofit
    organization that works to prevent gun violence
    by drafting, passing, and implementing
    legislation. The organization also takes a tough
    stance against the NRA and advocates against
    agendas that make it easy for guns to end up in
    the wrong hands.

Everytown for Gun Safety
(646) 324-8250
Website: https://everytown.org
Facebook and Twitter: @Everytown
Everytown for Gun Safety is a movement that aims
    to end gun violence and make communities safer.

Moms Demand Action for Gun Sense
Website: https://momsdemandaction.org
Facebook: @MomsDemandAction
Twitter: @MomsDemand
Moms Demand Action for Gun Sense was created
    by mothers after the Sandy Hook School
    shooting to pressure lawmakers and politicians

to support sensible gun-law reform. The website provides information about getting involved with preventing gun violence nationwide.

Sandy Hook Promise
13 Church Hill Road
Newtown, CT 06470
Website: https://www.sandyhookpromise.org
Facebook: @SandyHookPromise
Twitter: @SandyHook
Sandy Hook Promise is a nonprofit organization started by parents who lost children during the Sandy Hook massacre. It provides programs and resources to protect and prevent children from encountering gun violence.

Stop Handgun Violence
12 Broadway
Beverly, MA 01915
Website: http://www.stophandgunviolence.org
Facebook: @StopHandGunViolence
Twitter: @StopHandGuns
Stop Handgun Violence is an organization that aims to eradicate gun violence by educating the public, pushing for gun reform, and supporting law enforcement without banning guns.

For Further Reading

Cefrey, Holly. *Gun Violence*. New York, NY: Rosen Publishing, 2009.

Cook, Philip J., and Kristin A. Goss. *The Gun Debate: What Everyone Needs to Know.* New York: Oxford University Press: 2014.

Croft, Jennifer. *Everything You Need to Know About Guns in Your Home*. New York, NY: Rosen Publishing, 2000.

Cunningham, Anne C. *Critical Perspectives on Gun Control*. New York, NY: Enslow Publishing, 2017.

Furgang, Adam. Everything You Need to Know About Gun Violence. New York, NY: Rosen Publishing, 2018.

Hubbard, Jenny. *And We Stay*. New York, NY: Delacorte Press, 2014.

Jost, Kenneth. *Gun Violence: Are Stronger Measures Needed to Protect Society?* Washington, DC: Congressional Quarterly, 2007.

Magoon, Kekla. *How It Went Down*. New York, NY: Square Fish, Henry Holt and Company, 2015.

Merino, Noel. *Opposing Viewpoints: Gun Violence*. New York, NY: Greenhaven Press, 2015.

Moore, David Barclay. *The Stars Beneath Our Feet*. New York, NY: Alfred A. Knopf, 2017.

Nakaya, Andrea. *Thinking Critically: Mass Shootings*. San Diego, CA: ReferencePoint Press, 2013.

Nijkamp, Marieke. *This Is Where It Ends*. Naperville, IL: Sourcebooks Fire, 2016.

Reynolds, Jason. *Long Way Down*. New York, NY: Simon & Schuster, 2018.

Scherer, Lauri S. *Gun Violence*. New York, NY: Greenhaven Press, 2013.

Thomas, Angie. *The Hate U Give*. New York, NY: Balzer + Bray, 2017.

Wolny, Philip. *Gun Rights: Interpreting the Constitution*. New York, NY: Rosen Publishing, 2018.

Bibliography

Aizenman, Nurith. "Gun Violence: How The U.S. Compares With Other Countries." NPR, October 6, 2017. www.npr.org/sections /goatsandsoda/2017/10/06/555861898/gun -violence-how-the-u-s-compares-to-other -countries.

Azrael, D., C. Barber, and J. Mercy. "Linking data to save lives: Recent progress in establishing a National Violent Death Reporting System." *Harvard Health Policy Review* 2, January 2001: 38-42.

Baker, Jeanine, and Samara McPhedran. "Gun Laws and Sudden Death: Did the Australian Firearm Legislation of 1996 Make a Difference?" *British Journal of Criminology*, October 18, 2006.

Chapman, S. et al. "Australia's 1996 gun law reforms: Faster fall in firearm deaths, firearm suicides, and a decade without mass shootings." *Injury Prevention* 12, December 2006: 365–72

CNN Wire. "Dylann Roof Confesses to Killing 9 People in Charleston Church, Wanting to Start Race War." Myfox8.com, June 19, 2015. http:// myfox8.com/2015/06/19/charleston-shooting -suspect-dylan-roof-confesses-to-killing-9 -people.

Conner, Tracy, et al. "Light amidst the darkness: Heroic teacher Victoria Soto remembered." NBCNews.com, December 19, 2012. http:// usnews.nbcnews.com.

Crane, Emily. "Teenager Is Hailed a Hero after She Helped Thwart Another High School Shooting by Alerting Police When Her 18-Year-Old Friend Texted Her about His Plans to Carry out an Attack." *Daily Mail*, February 25, 2018. www.dailymail.co.uk/news/article-5423927/Teen-reveals-helped-thwart-Vermont-high-shooting.html.

Dahlberg, Linda L. et al. "Guns in the Home and Risk of a Violent Death in the Home: Findings from a National Study." *American Journal of Epidemiology*, November 15, 2004.

Donohue, et al. "Right-to-Carry Laws and Violent Crime: A Comprehensive Assessment Using Panel Data, the LASSO, and a State-Level Synthetic Controls Analysis." National Bureau of Economic Research, June 2017. http://www.nber.org/papers/w23510.

Hardy, Marjorie S. "Behavior-Oriented Approaches to Reducing Youth Gun Violence." *The Future of Children*, vol. 12, no. 2, Summer–Autumn, 2002.

Hickey, Walter. "How The Gun Industry Funnels Tens Of Millions Of Dollars To The NRA." *Business Insider*, January 16, 2013, http://www.businessinsider.com/gun-industry-funds-nra-2013-1.

Horn, Dan. "Gun Buybacks Popular but Ineffective, Experts Say." *USA Today*, January

13, 2013. https://www.usatoday.com/story/news /nation/2013/01/12/gun-buybacks-popular-but -ineffective/1829165.

Jacobson, Louis. "More Americans Killed by Guns since 1968 than in all U.S. Wars, columnist Nicholas Kristof writes." Politifact, August 27, 2015. http:// www.politifact.com/punditfact/statements/2015 /aug/27/nicholas-kristof/more-americans -killed-guns-1968-all-wars-says-colu.

Lyons, Saralyn. "Tale of Two Baltimores: Experts Discuss Roots of City Health Disparities." Hub, April 14, 2016. https://hub.jhu.edu/2016/04/14 /redlining-baltimore-public-health-disparities.

Parker, Kim, et al. "The Demographics of Gun Ownership." Pew Research Center: Social & Demographic Trends, June 22, 2017. http:// www.pewsocialtrends.org.

Pfefferbaum, B. e al. "Media exposure in children one hundred miles from a terrorist bombing." *Annals of Clinical Psychiatry* 15, March 2003: 1–8.

Scheu, Katherine. "Timothy Batts Offers Daughter's Last Words: 'Daddy, Just Tell Me It's a Dream.'" *Tennessean*, June 19, 2017. Retrieved on February 25, 2018. http://www.tennessean.com ./story/news/crime/2017/07/19/live-updates -trial-timothy-batts-accused-shooting-and -killing-daughter-timea/491278001.

Shepard, Steven. "Gun Control Support Surges in Polls." Politico, February 28, 2018. https://www.politico.com/story/2018/02/28/gun-control-polling-parkland-430099.

Smith, David. "Trump's Solution to School Shootings: Arm Teachers with Guns." Guardian.com, February 21, 2018. https://www.theguardian.com/us-news/2018/feb/21/donald-trump-solution-to-school-shootings-arm-teachers-with-guns.

Index

About the Author

Tiffanie Drayton is a writer and activist from Jersey City, New Jersey. She runs programs to keep at-risk children in urban communities off of the streets and away from guns. Her work advocating for social justice has been featured in many publications and is often used in university curricula. You can reach out to her on Twitter: @draytontiffanie.

Photo Credits

Cover Drew Angerer/Getty Images; p. 5 Robert Hoetink /Shutterstock.com; pp. 8–9 Sandy Huffaker/Corbis News /Getty Images; p. 11 Rich Legg/E+/Getty Images; pp. 14–15 OcusFocus /iStock/Thinkstock; pp. 18–19 DPA Picture Alliance/Alamy Stock Photo; pp. 22–23 Karl Sonnenberg/Shutterstock.com; p. 25 New York Daily News Archive/Getty Images; p. 27 Ullstein Bild/Getty Images; pp. 30–31 Rena Schild/Shutterstock.com; pp. 34–35 Rodimov /Shutterstock.com; p. 39 Anatoly Vartanov/Shutterstock.com; p. 40 Andrew Zarivny/Shutterstock.com; pp. 44–45 Barcroft Media /Getty Images; pp. 46–47 Leigh Vogel/WireImage/Getty Images; pp. 50–51 Slaven Vlasic/Getty Images; pp. 52–53 Orlando Sentinel /Tribune News Service/Getty Images; pp. 56–57 Joe Raedle /Getty Images; pp. 60–61 Odua Images/Shutterstock.com; p. 64 Bowdenimages/iStock/Thinkstock; pp. 66–67 © AP Images; pp. 68–69 Alexandre Marchi/Gamma-Rapho/Getty Images; pp. 72–73 Javi Indy/Shutterstock.com; pp. 76–77 Boston Globe/Getty Images; pp. 78–79 Pacific Press/LightRocket/Getty Images; pp. 84–85 Don Juan Moore/Getty Images; pp. 86–87 David Tran Photo/Shutterstock.com; pp. 92–93 Bloomberg/Getty Images; pp. 94–95 Rhona Wise/AFP /Getty Images.

Design and Layout: Nicole Russo-Duca; Editor: Rachel Aimee; Photo Researcher: Sherri Jackson